FATHER NUGE S
LIVERPOOL
1849 - 1905

by

Patricia Runaghan

Father Nugent

First Published 2003 by Countyvise Limited, 14 Appin Road, Birkenhead, Wirral CH41 9HH

Copyright © 2003 Patricia Runaghan

The right of Patricia Runaghan to be identified as the author of this work has been asserted by her in accordance with the Copyright, Design and Patents Act 1988.

British Library Cataloguing in Publication Data.
A catalogue record for this book is available from the British Library.

ISBN 1 901231 39 9

All rights reserved. No part of this publication may be reproduced, stored in a retrieval system, or transmitted, in any other form, or by any other means, electronic, chemical, mechanic, photocopying, recording or otherwise, without the prior permission of the publisher.

The Rev. Father Nugent

Father Nugent

Acknowledgements

I would like to thank the following for their help:

Pat McEvoy and Andy Wood of the Nugent Care Society, Paul Shaw and the Generalate Archives of the Poor Servants of the Mother of God, the staff of the Liverpool Records Office and the Liverpool Maritime Museum.

1

The Beginning

Of the many great men and women who were born in Liverpool, one name has, to a certain degree, been overlooked. It is that of a Catholic priest, Father James Nugent. Yet, in the second half of the 19th century, there can have been scarcely a household in the city which did not know and respect his name.

Apart from a biography written by Canon J Bennett in 1949, from which the following details have been taken, very little has been written about Fr Nugent.

He was born on 3rd March 1822 in Hunter Street, Liverpool, the eldest of the nine children of John and Mary Nugent, nee Rice, and baptised at St Nicholas' Pro Cathedral, Copperas Hill, on 17th March. Hunter Street was situated below William Brown Street, then known as Shaw's Brow. It ran between Byrom Street and Christian Street. It has long since disappeared, as has St Nicholas' Church.

James's father was an Irishman, from County Meath. He owned a poulterer's shop, and a stall in St John's Market. His wife was a convert to Catholicism.

James attended a private school in Queen's Square, as educational facilities for Catholics were very restricted. He was intended for a business career in the office of W G Maxwell and Co, King Street, Liverpool, but fortunately his parents first consulted their local priest, who thought that James showed signs of a vocation to the priesthood.

THE BIRTHPLACE OF MONSIGNOR NUGENT,
22 HUNTER-STREET, LIVERPOOL.
(From Photo by College Photo Co., Boundary-place.)

After eight years of study, first at Ushaw, and later at the English College, Rome, James returned home to Liverpool to be ordained at St Nicholas' Church by Bishop George Brown, possibly the first priest ever to be ordained there. His first parish was St Alban's, Blackburn. His first recorded sermon, in 1847, was preached in aid of the Liverpool Famine Fund: it raised £72.12s.8d. He was soon called back to St Nicholas' as a curate in January 1849, to replace Fr Robert Gillow, who had died of typhus fever.

The Liverpool to which Fr Nugent returned, as a newly ordained priest, was reeling from the effects of the Irish Famine and the typhus epidemic that followed. During the summer of 1849, 5,000 would die from cholera. Fr Nugent was one of the 35 Catholic priests in the borough who risked their lives visiting the sick and dying Irish poor.

Pauper Catholics were being buried in the parish burial grounds of the Established Church, ten bodies to a grave, in St Mary's, Cambridge Street and St Michael's, Kent Street, their priests unable to officiate

Metal figures representing famine victims at North Wall Quay, Dublin, where they would have boarded the "coffin ships" bound for Liverpool.

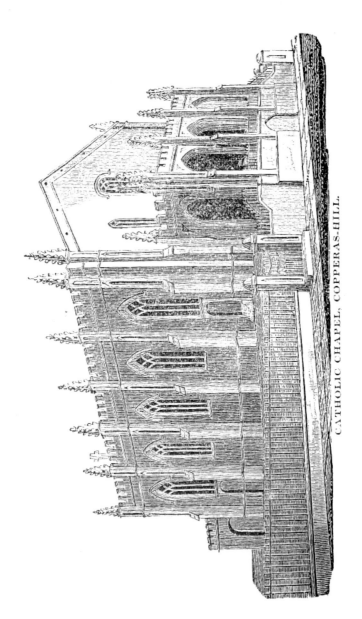

CATHOLIC CHAPEL, COPPERAS-HILL.

Line drawing of St Nicholas' Chapel, Courtesy of the Liverpool Records Office, Liverpool Libraries

at their burial. Later in the century, two municipal cemeteries were established, at Anfield and Toxteth Park.
Liverpool's already acute housing shortage had been exacerbated by the influx of Irish immigrants, many simply passing through on their way to North America, but a large minority too poor or too sick to get any further. They arrived by steam-packet at Clarence Dock. From there it was but a short walk to Vauxhall Road and its slums. They filled the courts and alleys, and the already condemned cellars in the poorest areas near the docks, in Vauxhall, St Paul's and Exchange wards to the north and Pitt Street and Toxteth to the south.

In 1841, the population of Liverpool was almost 300,000; by 1851 it had leapt to 376,000. Of this total, some 22% were Irish born, a majority coming from the province of Leinster, and over half of these from County Dublin.[1] In his book[2] Frank Neal estimates that the Liverpool Irish, ie the immigrants and their children, totalled around 90,000, or 24% of the total population.

As he went about the town, Fr Nugent could not help being aware of the vast numbers of homeless and parentless children. They haunted the streets, begging and stealing in order to exist, and sleeping in boxes and under bridges at night. 64 out of every 100 would die before the age of nine, from preventable causes.[3] These were the people among whom he was to work for the next 50 years.

Fr Nugent had a love-hate relationship with the Liverpool-Irish; he wanted to be proud of them, but they kept letting him down. He once referred to them as 'the dregs'. On the other hand, he was a close friend of John Denvir, a leading member of the Irish Republican Brotherhood, forerunner of the IRA. But despite this, Fr Nugent had no interest in politics, and he was criticised by local Nationalists for not joining the Home Rule campaign, religion and politics being inseparable.

He was convinced that the long-term solution to child poverty and homelessness lay in education, and this inspired him to set up a Catholic Middle School in Rodney Street, followed by the Catholic Institute in Hope Street. In the years that followed he was to be instrumental in setting up orphanages, training schools, mother-and-baby homes, and hostels for single working men and women.

Fr Nugent's pioneering social work was often reported in the local press, both Tory and Liberal, at first critically, but with increasing approbation as time went on.

NOTES

1. T Burke: *Catholic History of Liverpool* (1910) p171.
2. F Neal: *Sectarian Violence - The Liverpool Experience 1819 - 1914* (1988) p11.
3. Burke: p82.

Duke's Terrace
Liverpool's last remaining back to back houses,
Now being restored.

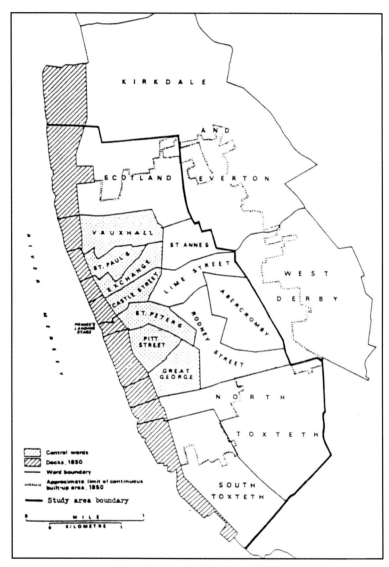

The political wards of the borough 1851

1851 CENSUS

DRYDEN STREET AREA, VAUXHALL, LIVERPOOL.

TABLE 1.

PLACES OF BIRTH (total registered population 583)

	Liverpool	Lancs.	Cheshire	Ireland	Wales	Scotland	Rest of England	Isle of Man	Rest of World
STEWART	49	8	6	7	0	1	7	0	0
JONES	29	5	1	138	1	1	3	2	0
OWENS	49	9	4	16	2	1	2	0	0
THOMAS	66	3	2	8	0	0	2	0	0
DRYDEN	51	2	1	11	2	2	15	1	2
YORK	33	3	7	22	2	3	3	0	0
TOTAL	277	30	21	202	7	8	32	3	2

TABLE 2

PLACES OF BIRTH (Head of Household)

	Liverpool	Lancs.	Cheshire	Ireland	Wales	Scotland	Rest of England	Isle of Man	Rest of World
STEWART	8	5	1	2	0	1	2	0	2
JONES	3	1	0	17	1	0	2	0	0
OWENS	7	4	1	4	2	0	0	0	0
THOMAS	12	2	0	5	0	0	1	0	0
DRYDEN	4	0	0	4	0	1	5	1	0
YORK	4	1	1	5	1	2	0	0	0
TOTAL	38	13	3	37	4	4	10	1	0

TOTAL 111 Heads of Household.

8

2
Poor Schools vs Ragged Schools

In 1826, Liverpool Corporation had provided two schools in order that the poorest children should have some form of elementary education; this was 44 years before the Education Act of 1870 made it compulsory. The North Corporation School was situated in Bevington Bush, and the South Corporation School was in Park Lane. There was a charge of 1½d per child, per week. However, the school's curriculum was taken over by the Established Church and all Catholic children were withdrawn by their parents.[1]

Three months after his arrival in Liverpool in 1849, Fr Nugent had preached at the opening of Holy Cross temporary school in Standish Street. The sight of so many destitute children pouring into the school affected him profoundly. To him, education was the first step on the road to self-respect and prosperity. He decided there and then to try and persuade one of the teaching orders of nuns to come to Liverpool to take charge of a Poor School at St Nicholas' in order to provide a basic standard of education for the children there.

On 28th March 1851, six Sisters of Notre Dame, all Belgians, arrived in Liverpool from Blackburn in response to Fr Nugent's invitation. On their arrival they drove to the house which had been taken for them at No 3 Islington Flags. They found it in great confusion, men putting up bedsteads, women scrubbing floors.

Later in the afternoon Fr Nugent arrived, accompanied by Rev Fr Worthy, parish priest of St Nicholas', and Fr Carr. They began to prepare dinner for the sisters.

'It was curious to see these good priests so actively employed in the cooking department. Being Friday, the dinner consisted of fried soles, potatoes, and rice pudding. After cooking dinner, the reverend gentlemen left, Fr Worthy returning later to discuss the new school.'

Sister Superior described the condition of St Nicholas' Poor School when she first saw it as:

'One large room with a gallery at one end, for the infants. The other children arranged in little square classes, from 20 to 30 each class, under the care of a pupil teacher. We found great disorder prevailing throughout, as there had been no mistress for some time.'[2]

Fr Nugent had his critics among the clergy. They predicted that the experiment would be a failure. Twelve months later HM Inspector of Schools gave St Nicholas' a glowing report, both for its educational and its moral standards.

Fr Nugent's success at St Nicholas' was an inspiration to the clergy of the recently built church of St Francis Xavier in Shaw Street, who were facing a similar problem. They could expect no help from their parishioners, the poverty-stricken Famine immigrants who had not yet shaken off the terrors of 1847. Fr O'Carroll, curate, estimated that there were not less than 60,000 poor Catholic children in the city who were receiving no education whatsoever.[3]

In a petition to the Privy Council for a grant towards the erection of a Poor School,[4] Fr O'Carrol's reasons show how desperate the situation was:

'Great numbers of distressed settlers from Ireland whose children, unless in school, become frequently lost on the streets; there is no Catholic school within practicable distance of St Francis Xavier Church, around which great numbers of the poorer classes have settled, and are daily settling, in the small new streets that are being erected, the houses in which are all let before they are finished;[5] that 500 children, almost

St Francis Xavier's Church, Shaw Street,
Courtesy of the Liverpool Records Office, Liverpool Libraries

wholly destitute of instruction, flock each Sunday to the church, which the clergy are obliged to turn into a school; that your lordships have given large assistance to St Austin's Edge Lane (C of E), only a few yards away. This class of Catholics are far more destitute.'[6]

It was customary to solicit alms for the new schools that were so badly needed; from the pennies of the poor, to the more substantial donations of the city's prominent Catholic businessmen. On one such occasion, as Fr O'Carroll approached the Wavertree office of a well-known and generous benefactor, he was dismayed to see the retreating figure of Fr Nugent, who had obviously just left the premises on a similar mission.

It was thanks to this generosity that the first stone of the new school was laid, in1853, by Alderman Richard Sheil, a Liverpool Irishman and Liberal councillor (Sheil Road is named after him). The school was formally opened the following year, and staffed by the Sisters of Mercy.

Once St Francis Xavier Poor School was up and running, the Sisters organised free meals for its half-starved pupils. This was necessary both for the children's survival, and in order to tempt them to attend daily. Meals were served to about 150 children per day. There were conditions, of course. In order to qualify, a child must have attended 10am Mass on the previous Sunday. This condition must have disqualified quite a number of hungry children, for whom Saturday nights brought only abuse from drunken parents.

Those who qualified queued with a tin plate and a mug. A sample of the meals shows that it was probably the most nourishing of the day for many children: Monday and Thursday - 'scouse', ie potatoes, meat and vegetables. Tuesday - meat with pea soup. Wednesday - pudding made of dripping, bread, sugar, flour, currants and raisins. Friday - no meat allowed, of course, but boiled rice and milk. The average cost per meal, per child, was one farthing. Apparently, the poorer the child, the more fastidious, even though some had fainted through weakness or hunger.

Free clothing was also distributed to the poorest pupils, but the children were told publicly that the items were only lent, in order to prevent drunken parents from pawning them, after one mother had been detected, who pawned for a drink in the afternoon, a new flannel petticoat given to her child in the morning.

Ragged schools were first introduced by the Church of England in the 1840s. By 1851 there were 26 of them in Liverpool.[6] They were more a means of getting children off the streets than of giving them any real education. Their stated objective was to 'rescue young persons from a state of present destitution and incipient vice, and thus prevent them from becoming confirmed criminals.' They soon became a cause of friction.

The Catholic clergy believed they were run by 'blanket and soup' Protestants, ie that they were trying to convert poor Catholic children by offering them clothes and soup. Their efforts were to be counteracted by Catholics coming forward and providing the means of educating their own children. Fr. Pierse Power, of St. Patrick's church, Toxteth, had visited his local Ragged School, and insisted on withdrawing some of the children on the grounds that their faith was in danger.[8] Thus the idea of segregated education in Liverpool was born.

Canon Abraham Hume was vicar in charge of St Stephen's C of E church in Byrom Street. In 1850 he undertook a survey of St Stephen's and Vauxhall ecclesiastical districts. He was helped in the task by his scripture readers of whom there were, at the time, 40 - 50 under the auspices of the Anglican Church. They visited the poor in their homes in order to instruct them in spiritual affairs. Some held open-air preaching sessions, which were frequently a cause of public disturbances in this divided city.

As well as evaluating the religious observances, Canon Hume's survey highlighted the awful lack of education for the many thousands of children in his area. He estimated that, in 1850, 2092 children in Vauxhall district were receiving no education at all, out of a school-age population of over 3200,[9] the only school existing in north Liverpool at that time being at St Mary's Catholic chapel.

Finding suitable accommodation for such large numbers of children was not an easy task, but Canon Hume's lay-readers succeeded in opening two temporary day schools in a house, 63 Gascoyne Street, off Vauxhall Road. Each room accommodated 80 - 100 children, all of whom were expected to pay for their education.

For those for whom even the few pennies charged per week were out of the question, there were two free evening Ragged Schools held on the same premises. Here, the most destitute were taught on the first four evenings each week. On Friday evening there was a sermon, and Saturday was set apart for cleaning the premises - by the pupils, of course. Average attendance was about 60 boys and 34 girls.

Finding teachers was a problem. Canon Hume could not call upon an Order of Nuns as could Fr Nugent. He hoped to recruit young people who would give their spare time freely to this worthwhile cause, for example, educated mechanics or respectable business people. Meanwhile, he managed by using older pupils to help his lay-readers.

Canon Hume had the novel idea of distributing copies of the New Testament in Irish, ostensibly in an effort to lure Irish Protestants to his church, but as they formed only one in 100 of the local population, it was impossible to form a congregation.[10] As Irish Protestants, mainly from Ulster, spoke English, it was also a waste of time.

'Give the child a fair chance' was the rallying cry of Rev Thomas Major Lester, vicar of St Mary's Church, Kirkdale. In 1856, driven by the same compassion as the three preceding clergymen, he set up a Ragged Mission Room over, of all things, a coal shed, in Kirkdale.

Realising that it was futile to try to educate half-starved children, he tried to induce them by offering a free meal. Of course, such a contentious move was bound to be interpreted by the Catholic clergy as 'damning their souls for penny rowls and flitches of hairy bacon.'[11] Major Lester continued to work unceasingly for the education and welfare of thousands of destitute urchins who roamed the city's slum-ridden streets. In 1862 he opened Kirkdale Ragged School, and in 1864, a girls' home in Walton Road. He died in 1903. His statue complements that of Mgr Nugent in St John's Gardens, Liverpool.

You could be forgiven for thinking that only the clergy were interested in education in Liverpool, and even they were unable to work in harmony. In fact, the secular authorities were locked in combat over the subject during the second half of the 19th century. As the number of Irish immigrants in the town increased, so the education of their children became a political and religious battleground. 'The Times' of 26th July 1848 expressed the view of many English citizens: 'Every hard-working man in this country carries a whole Irish family on his back.'

The Liverpool Liberal Party, at first champions of the immigrants' rights, found that this policy was losing them seats on the Town Council, as the anti-Irish policies of the Conservative Party found popular support, and kept it. As Liberal influence waned, its place was taken by the Irish Nationalist Party.

NOTES

1. In 1807 the Benevolent Society of St Patrick had founded Pleasant Street School to provide an education for Irish children, regardless of their religious   background.
2. *Foundations of the Sisters of Notre Dame in England and Scotland from 1845   - 1895* (1895) p47.
3. *'Xaverian'* (1853) p12 Schooling was not compulsory before 1870.
4. The Privy Council was willing to contribute, providing the school taught what we would now call the national curriculum.

5. As these newly-built houses extended northward, the building standard deteriorated until they merged into courts, alleys and back-to-back housing, equal to the worst slum districts.
6. *'Exaverian'* p13.
7. *Liverpool Courier*, 24th July 1851.
8. *Liverpool Courier*, 23rd February 1853.
9. Canon Abraham Hume: *Missions at Home, or a Clergyman's Account of the Town of Liverpool* (1850) p26.
10. In 1851 there was one Reformed Irish Presbyterian Church in Liverpool, with   seating for 120. *Religious Worship in 1851*, from *Parliamentary Papers 1852   - 1853.*
11. Thomas Burke: *Catholic History of Liverpool* (1910) p108, A humorous

Remaining boundary wall of former St. Mary's burial ground in Cambridge street/ Mulberry Street. The bricked-up square was originally open. Bodies could be pushed through here, after the gates were locked at night.

song   of the time.

Holy Cross Church, Courtesy of the Liverpool Records Office, Liverpool Libraries

Courtesy of the Liverpool Records Office, Liverpool Libraries

3

Housing the Poor - Lace Street

In 1846, the Borough Council had appointed Dr William Duncan as first Medical Officer of Health. His first report came as no surprise. He estimated that 70% of the population of the borough of Liverpool were 'working poor' and that half of these (76,000) were living in crowded, insanitary courts, with a single water supply and an earth privy. Rents varied between two shillings and ninepence, and four shillings and sixpence per week, according to how near the open cesspool and privy.[1]

Houses were mostly three storeys high, with one or two rooms per storey. The rear room received no direct light as the houses backed onto those in the next court. Rooms were let singly. Some houses had cellars, often with a mud floor. Despite these cellars having been cleared, they had filled up again with desperate migrants, a whole family occupying just one room.

Lace Street was typical of housing in the Vauxhall area. Its grim exterior concealed the entrances to atrocious courts and cellars. In 1850 - 1851, the population of this short street and its adjoining twenty-five courts was a staggering 1,110 persons, comprising 179 families of whom 153, or 85.5% were Irish speaking.[2]

Baptisms at nearby Holy Cross church, Standish Street, during 1851, (its first full year - it was built in 1850) of children born in Lace Street alone totalled 45, to the 89 families in the street, or one birth for every alternate family. No doubt some were baptised elsewhere, and others not at all.

St Martin-in-the-Fields was an Anglican church situated in Sylvester Street, whose adjoining burial ground was used for pauper burials after 1847, when St Mary's cemetery in Cambridge Street was filled. Today it is a recreation ground, and St Mary's is a college car park.

Burials at St Martin's for the same year, 1851, of residents of Lace Street totalled 32, 28 being described as Romanists, and presumably Irish. The youngest was aged one day, the oldest 47 years. These figures confirm the evidence of the 1851 census, that it was, above all, young people who left Ireland during the Famine; the old stayed behind to die.

However unacceptable, these figures were an improvement on previous years. For example, in 1847 one third of the inhabitants of Lace Street and its courts (472 persons) died from fever.[3] The high rate of mortality in the Vauxhall area as a whole could be mainly attributed to the defective sanitary conditions that prevailed at the time. Lace Street had three water pumps, to serve its entire population, the water being turned on only at certain times of the day and night.

Prior to the introduction in 1846 of guano as a manure[4] the nightsoil men not only emptied the middens and ashpits regularly, free of charge, but also paid the Borough Council for the privilege. Since then the nightmen had refused to do their job unless they were paid by the council.

The purpose of the Sanitary Amendment Act of 1864 was to open up the closed and confined courts, and to get rid of the midden system by converting as quickly as possible all privies into water closets.[5]

Of the occupants of these slums, Canon Hume, an Anglican clergyman, estimated that less than half were in regular employment, and those mostly as labourers or street traders. The remainder pursued unlawful occupations, eg 'men catchers' (persons who preyed on immigrants), bands of 'prigs' (juvenile thieves), poachers, professional smugglers and dog stealers. The poor showed only sympathy for criminals.

Burlington Street, Court Number 6, Courtesy of the Liverpool Records Office, Liverpool Libraries

No. 2 Court Silvester Street, July 1913. Courtesy of the Liverpool Records Office, Liverpool Libraries
Note the narrow, tunnel entrance to the court from the street. The top end of the court is closed, preventing light and air from entering. The lower walls are lime washed, in an attempt to disinfect them.

The returned convict was a 'young man who has been abroad, God help him.' The women who 'skinned' poor sailors (robbed them of not only their money, but of every article of clothing) were 'clever girls, and serve them just right.'

No activity could be hidden from neighbours living in such close proximity as this, and the minutest incidents were known to every resident. 'In one court in Vauxhall district, containing seven homes', wrote Canon Hume, 'there are five houses of ill-fame. Some streets are a terror to a solitary policeman, and into which a respectable person rarely ventures.'[6] Fr Nugent observed: 'I am often in the habit, of a Sunday afternoon, of coming down Vauxhall Road and Marybone, and I find these girls standing at the corners of all the streets. If you go into some of the public houses in Marybone, you will meet a large number of these girls there. If a labouring man marries one of these women, his home becomes neglected, and the children are allowed to prowl round the streets.'[7]

In 1883, a survey was undertaken by the 'Liverpool Daily Post' newspaper. Entitled 'Squalid Liverpool' it described the city's court-ridden streets as 'fever dens' and drew the attention of Liverpool's citizens to the situation that existed in their midst. Even so, the last of the 19th century's slums was demolished well into the 20th century.

Even the slums of Lace Street were beyond the reach of some. Yet the workhouse was seen as a last resort. The poor regarded the term 'pauper' as a degradation. Brownlow Hill workhouse was the largest in England, where the very poorest Irish migrants went. Parents were separated from their children, husbands from their wives. However, admittance was by no means automatic. An applicant was admitted by a written order from the Select Vestry, which had to be signed by an overseer of the poor.

There was an even lower class of pauper in this class-conscious society. Casual vagrants were admitted, at the discretion of the Master or Matron, to the vagrant sheds, segregated from their fellow paupers.

Liverpool Workhouse Aerial View, Courtesy of the Liverpool Records Office, Liverpool Libraries

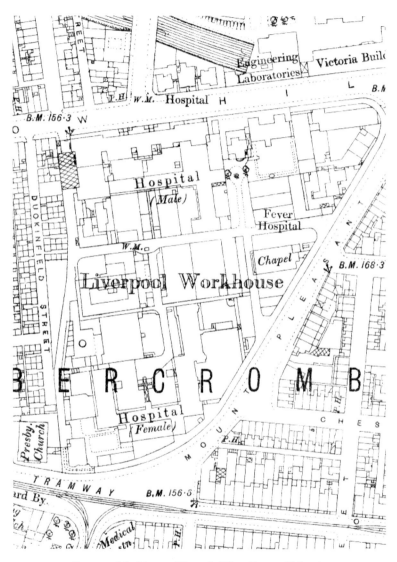

Courtesy of the Liverpool Records Office, Liverpool Libraries

The journalist Hugh Shimmin described the scene: 'A wayfarer arrives at the workhouse, tired and hungry, having walked for many miles. But first he must take a bath. Then he must grind 30lbs of corn to earn his meal, and this could take more than three hours. Only then is he allowed a tin of gruel and a hunk of bread as payment. His bed in the vagrant ward has a wooden pillow, his coverings are his own rags.'[8] His only crime was his poverty; he would have been treated better in prison.

During the year 1851, there were 135 baptisms of children born in the Liverpool workhouse, at St Nicholas' church, Copperas Hill, the nearest Catholic church. In the same year, the number of burials of inmates, at St Martin-in-the-Fields, Sylvester Street, totalled 661 of which approximately half were described as Romanist, and presumably Irish. Their ages ranged from one day to 79 years. But these figures lose their meaning when compared to those during the cholera epidemic of 1849.

In 1855, there were 3,317 paupers in the workhouse, of whom 1,245 were registered as Catholic, including 143 children under five.[9] No religious instruction was provided for them, and the 'leakage' rate was correspondingly high. The Select Vestry refused to allow Catholic services inside the workhouse, with the result that those able-bodied paupers who wished to hear Mass went outside on Sunday mornings, including a number who declared themselves Catholic for the day in order to smuggle out quantities of clothing, bed-linen etc. They returned in the evening, intoxicated, and disturbed the wards by their noisy behaviour.

After an enquiry, and a lot of opposition, a room was set aside for Catholic services, and a priest was allowed inside to instruct the children. Fr Nugent, who at this time was residing at the Catholic Institute at the corner of Hope Street and Maryland Street, just a few yards from Brownlow Hill, was the obvious choice. He was, by now, at the forefront of the Catholic clergy, full of restless energy, and highly thought of by Bishop Gross.

NOTES

1. Hugh Shimmin: *Liverpool Life,* 2nd series (1857) pp57 - 63.
2. Hume: pp14 - 15 The Irish language was a barrier to employment in an English-speaking world.
3. Burke: pp84 - 85.
4. Seabird droppings, arriving by the shipload from Peru.
5. It is a measure of Fr Nugent's growing influence that his opinion was asked   by the Committee as to the advantages of the wc in comparison with the   earth privy.
6. Hume: p18.
7. Liverpool Council Proceedings: Prison Minister's Report (1866) p198.
8. P(
9. B\

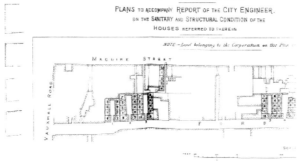

CITY OF LIVERPOOL.

PLANS TO ACCOMPANY REPORT OF THE CITY ENGINEER,
ON THE SANITARY AND STRUCTURAL CONDITION OF THE
HOUSES REFERRED TO THEREIN

NOTE—Land belonging to the Corporation on this Plan

Court and cellar dwellings in Toxteth and Vauxhall wards.

Source – Report of the City Engineer 1865.

		Breakfast			ADULTS *Dinner*								*Supper*	
		Thick Oatmeal Porridge	Skim Milk		Cooked Meat	Hashed Meat	Beef Scouse	Potatoe or Vegetables	Bread	Pea Soup	Soup	Suet Pudding	Bread	Milk Gruel
		pints	pints		oz	oz	lbs.	lbs.	oz	pints	pints	lbs.	oz	pints
Sunday	Men	2	¾			3		1½					8	2
	Women	1½	¾			3		1					7	1½
Monday	Men	2	¾									1½	8	2
	Women	1½	¾									1¼	7	1½
Tuesday	Men	2	¾		4			1½					8	2
	Women	1½	¾		4			1					7	1½
Wednesday	Men	2	¾						8		1		8	2
	Women	1½	¾						7		1		7	1½
Thursday	Men	2	¾			3		1½					8	2
	Women	1½	¾			3		1					7	1½
Friday	Men	2	¾						8	2			8	2
	Women	1½	¾						7	1½			7	1½
Saturday	Men	2	¾				2						8	2
	Women	1½	¾				1½						7	1½

CHILDREN														
		Thick Oatmeal Porridge	Skim Milk		Cooked Meat	Hashed Meat	Beef Scouse	Potatoe or Vegetables	Bread	Pea Soup	Soup	Suet Pudding	Bread	Milk Gruel
		pints	pints		oz	oz	lbs.	lbs.	oz	pints	pints	lbs.	oz	pints
Sunday	From 2 to 5 yrs	½	½			2		½					4	½
	5 to 9	1	¾			2½		¾					5	1
	9 to 16	1½	¾			3		1					7	1½
Monday	From 2 to 5 yrs	½	½									½	4	½
	5 to 9	1	¾									1	5	1
	9 to 16	1½	¾									1¾	7	1½
Tuesday	From 2 to 5 yrs	½	½		3			½					4	½
	5 to 9	1	¾		3½			¾					5	1
	9 to 16	1½	¾		4			1					7	1½
Wednesday	From 2 to 5 yrs	½	½						4		½		4	½
	5 to 9	1	¾						6		¾		5	1
	9 to 16	1½	¾						7		1		7	1½
Thursday	From 2 to 5 yrs	½	½		2			½					4	½
	5 to 9	1	¾		2½			¾					5	1
	9 to 16	1½	¾		3			1					7	1½
Friday	From 2 to 5 yrs	½	½						4	1			4	½
	5 to 9	1	¾						6	1			5	1
	9 to 16	1½	¾						7	1½			7	1½
Saturday	From 2 to 5 yrs	½	½				¾						4	½
	5 to 9	1	¾				1						5	1
	9 to 16	1½	¾				1½						7	1½

Suggested diets for the inmates of a workhouse,
Extracted from "The Guardians", Birkenhead Press 1974.

4
Save the Boy

As early as 1849, Fr Nugent had already experimented with the idea of establishing a Refuge to feed and shelter the poor Irish waifs who had begun to infest the streets of Liverpool. But it was in 1864 that he decided to set up a night-shelter for destitute boys at Spitalfields, off Whitechapel. He gave his reasons for doing so:

'If a destitute boy is left to take his chance upon the streets, in a few years he will be a man without principle, without morality, and as he has no honest way to get his living, he will prey on society and maintain himself by dishonesty ... we may strive in vain afterwards to reform him in gaol.'[1]

The Shelter was begun with the objective of taking in boys who would otherwise have spent the night huddled in doorways, cold and hungry. These were the children of the Irish immigrants who had arrived in Liverpool a decade ago and more. Now, only one in ten was Irish born.

On arrival they were each given a basin of coffee and half-a-pound of bread 'with a dash of treacle' for their supper. During 1867 the Shelter gave out 48,205 suppers and 2,913 nights' lodgings.[2] Admission was regardless of creed. It was this all-embracing charity that endeared Fr Nugent to all classes.

He soon came to realise that a night-shelter was not enough. What was needed was a permanent home where the boys could be taught a trade and prepared for adult life. At a public meeting in St George's Hall, he canvassed the support of clergymen of all persuasions to do all in their power to help him eradicate the scandal of destitute children from the town.

Helped by John Denvir, his 'right-hand man' who coined the phrase 'Save the Boy', Fr Nugent rented a tumbledown house at 22 - 24 Soho Street. The house was in a district with a high rate of drunkenness and crime. It was reputed to be haunted, a fact which enabled him to rent it more cheaply, because nobody else would live there.

Every night the house was crowded with destitute lads, so much so that they had to be let in by the front door and out by the back, They were given supper, a bed for the night if they needed it, and substantial breakfast in the morning. No one was turned away. There were provisions for 38 boys, but on one night 647 were provided with food.[3] 'Father Nujint' as they called him, begged for the money to buy food for his boys, from prominent businessmen in the town. They were taught to read and write, and to make their own boots and clothes. Later, he bought a printing press in order that the boys might be taught a trade. They were responsible for the printing of the 'Northern Press' and later, its successor the 'Catholic Times'. Father Nugent commented: 'It was no easy matter to train these wild, wayward lads, but with a religious foundation the rest of the work was slowly accomplished.' He had no time to be complacent; a census taken at midnight on 1st January 1869 found 541 little boys and 172 little girls on the streets, begging or trading small articles.[4]

Soon, larger premises were needed. In 1869, Fr Nugent acquired the elegant house in St Anne Street where the assize judges had lodged when in Liverpool. It was officially opened on 22nd July by Bishop Goss. The Refuge boys' band, of which he was justly proud, played on the (flat) roof on fine summer evenings, attracting a large crowd in the surrounding streets.[5] They even went on a tour of Ireland, accompanied by Fr Nugent, who delivered a lecture on 'Nobody's Children' which brought tears to the eyes of his audience. His critics said he had missed his vocation, and should have been an actor. However, the publicity surrounding his work was instrumental in bringing the Education Act of 1869 into existence.

After Fr Nugent's death, the Refuge continued to thrive. It was managed by a superintendent and a matron, and taught by the Sisters of Charity of St Paul, assisted by the Franciscan Friars of St Mary's, Fox Street. At the annual inspection of 1914, by HM Inspector of Reformatory and Industrial Schools, the managers were praised for their efforts for the boys' wellbeing. Good behaviour was encouraged and rewarded by letting boys go home for Christmas, and by the provision of a summer camp, at Moreton, on the Wirral peninsular.

There were 145 inmates, 20 boys having left during the year. All had been found employment by the school, and by using juvenile employment agencies. Fr Nugent's influence can be seen in the boys' choice of careers; four had been apprenticed as tailors, three had become printers, and one had joined an Army band.[6]

Old 'Refuge Boys' kept in touch, many coming from afar to attend the Old Boys' Annual Reunion in Liverpool.

Fr John Berry was Rector of St Philip Neri's Oratory, in Catharine Street. In 1892, following in Fr Nugent's footsteps, he opened a Refuge, St Philip's House, off Williamson Square, for street traders and destitute boys. He soon realised that because of their differing needs, they must be kept separate.

In order to discourage scroungers, Father Berry charged the street trading boys 2d per head for a bed, 2d for supper, and 2d for breakfast. But as the average wage of a street trader was assessed at only five shillings and twopence per week, it meant that he had nothing left for other needs. His clothes wear out - he is no longer respectable - he loses his job. Leave him alone, and he drifts into crime and ends up in gaol; treat him generously, and he takes advantage of every charitable effort. The only hope of saving him is to place him in a Training Home where he will be weaned from his old life. Fr Berry hoped to establish this Home, helped financially by Fr Nugent, who made over to him the 'Catholic Times'.

In 1894, Fr Berry opened a night-shelter for penniless lads. They paid for a warm bath, a bed and a meal, by performing small tasks, that they were obliged to do. But in 1897, the Shelter closed through lack of cash. By then it had given 4,271 meals, and 2,188 beds, admitting all, regardless of creed, in return for a small piece of work, in the spirit of Fr Nugent.

NOTES

1. LCP Prison Minister's Report (1866) p584. The first Industrial School Act came into force in 1857. It empowered magistrates to commit boys to schools holding an Industrial Schools Certificate, in order to protect them from becoming criminals. Fr. Nugent secured a certificate for the Boys' Refuge.
2. Bennett p40.
3. Burke p173.
4. Bennett p41.
5. Boy bands were a popular way of raising money. Canon Major Lester's Band of Boy Musicians also played in the surrounding streets.
6. St Anne Street RC Boys Industrial School, Annual Inspection (1914) p2.
7. *Cathedral Record*, vol IX (1949).

5
An Alternative to Gaol - The 'Clarence' Reformatory Ship

The scandal of children who were convicted of minor offences being sent to adult prisons roused Fr Nugent to seek an alternative.The Society of Friends had already opened the first reformatory school, which was a great success. The Liverpool Juvenile Reformatory Association had launched a training ship, the 'Akbar'. These initiatives had led to the Reformatory Schools Act of 1854, which authorised financial help for those institutions which accepted children convicted of crime.

The first meeting of the Liverpool Catholic Reformatory Association took place in 1864, with Fr Nugent as president. A proposal to establish a ship reformatory in the River Mersey, off New Ferry, had already been agreed in principle in 1858, when Cardinal Wiseman of Westminster, on a visit to Liverpool, had suggested a fact-finding tour of the Protestant reformatory ship, the 'Akbar', already moored in the Sloyne.

This was a '50-gun' frigate, fitted up as a training school for up to 150 destitute and delinquent boys, in order to train them for a 'maritime life'. The idea had already been tried in other parts of the country, under the direction of the Government, and reported to be a success. Cost of fitting out the ship was £1,500. Under the direction of the Liverpool Juvenile Reformatory Association, boys received three hours instruction daily from a schoolmaster. On Sundays they were sent to the floating church, Birkenhead, and on one day a month they were allowed visitors.

The Admiralty, approached by Fr Nugent, agreed to loan a 2,279 ton battleship, first launched in 1827, and called the Duke of Clarence. She was able to accommodate at least 250 boys, but was seldom filled to capacity. The ship began service in 1864, after a refit. Local Protestants were angered by the awarding of a grant of £1,500 by Liverpool Corporation towards the cost. The offences for which most of her inmates had been sentenced were vagrancy, thieving, begging, and like offences. They had been remanded in Walton gaol before joining the 'Clarence'.

TABLE 1   Number of juveniles arrested and tried for minor offences.

Year	Number
1860	768
1862	1,159
1864	1,299
1867	1,500

Source: T Burke, *Catholic History of Liverpool (1910) p167*

The task of reforming these young offenders began with teaching them to read and write. Fr Nugent was convinced that illiteracy was a factor which had been underestimated. The boys were taught to make their own boots and clothing, and of course they were taught seamanship. After three years or so the boys were released, and many were taken into the Merchant Navy.

TABLE 2   A return of the number of juveniles committed to
Walton   gaol, and ordered to be removed to the undermentioned reformatories during the year ending 30th September 1871, showing the number of times they have been previously in prison.

Name of reformatory	never before	once	twice	three times	total
Akbar	7	11	3	1	22

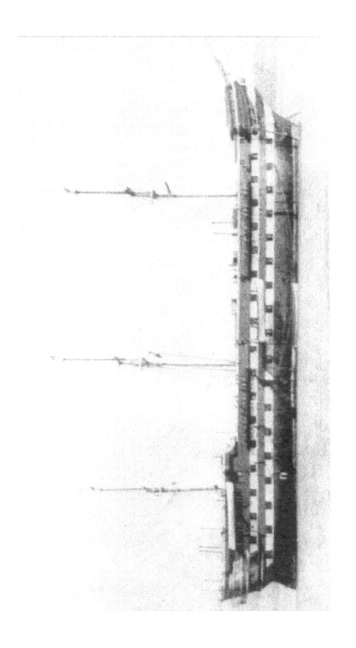

The 'Clarence' reformatory ship

Clarence	17	22	8	3	50

Source: *Liverpool Council Proceedings. Prison Minister's Report
     (1871) p592*
For twenty years all was well, but on 17th January 1884, the 'Clarence' was deliberately set on fire and burnt out. The six discontented boys responsible were sent to the assizes, and each sentenced to five years penal servitude. Fortunately, no lives were lost. The 'Liverpool Review' commented: 'How is it that other training ships in the river, containing exactly the same class of inmates, are kept under discipline without difficulty ... there should be no ill-judged leniency shown in their punishment.'[1]

A new 'Clarence' was brought into use in November 1885, and a tougher regime was introduced. However, in February 1886, there was a serious mutiny on board which ended with 13 boys being sent to the assizes, In July 1899, a group of boys managed to burn out the ship altogether, on the very night that the Bishop of Shrewsbury had arrived on board in preparation for a Confirmation service the next morning. The bishop and 235 boys and staff got away safely, but the fire spread so quickly that nothing could be saved. The Catholic Reformatory Association decided that enough was enough and established a nautical training school on dry land.

NOTES

1, *Liverpool Review* 19th January 1884.

6
Child Emigration - A Golden Opportunity?

Since 1850, emigration had been seen as a partial solution to unemployment, but when, in 1870, Fr Nugent took s group of 24 orphan children to Canada, it was probably the first organised emigration of its kind.

Before setting out, he had called a meeting of interested parties of all persuasions, including magistrates, Poor Law Guardians and others interested in child welfare, to explain his scheme. All the children were to be adopted by Canadian families, and Fr Nugent would use the opportunity to spend the following nine months on a lecture tour of Canada and the United States, pleading the cause of these children and raising money. This was a task at which he excelled. It was the first of many such visits. Although he urged local gentlemen to 'keep an eye on' the children's welfare, there was no real supervision.

In 1881, the Catholic Children's Protection Society was set up at 99 Shaw Street, Liverpool, precisely in order to carry on the work started by Fr Nugent, 'of rescuing orphan and abandoned children, and of placing them in comfortable homes in Canada, where they would have the opportunity of becoming useful and respectable members of the community.'[1]

Another, more urgent, reason for the establishment of the Society was that other organisations were already at work placing out children in North America, very many of them Catholics. The most prolific of these was Mrs Louisa Birt, the proprietor of Mrs Birt's Homes in Myrtle Street, Liverpool,who, in three years, had placed nearly 600 children on farms in Nova Scotia.[2]

Emigration to Canada 1884.
Courtesy of National Museums Liverpool (Merseyside Maritime Museum)

Mrs Birt had opened her first home in Bethnal Green, in London's East End, in 1868, helped by her two sisters, Annie and Rachel McPherson. Hearing of Liverpool's reputation as the 'Black Spot on the Mersey' and of the vast numbers of homeless and parentless children who roamed its streets, she arrived in the town in 1873. Her first Home was opened in Byrom Street, in one of the worst areas of the town, and with the highest infant mortality rate,

As a staunch Protestant, Mrs Birt felt that God had chosen her to do this work. Emigration seemed to be the only way of coping with the endless stream of deprived children who came to her. Firstly, they were given six months training in the Home in order to 'weed out the physical or morally unsuitable' (and we may wonder what befell these rejects).

A typical emigrant party would consist of: orphans - 23, motherless - 27, fatherless - 9, illegitimate - 5, parents living - 18, motherless, father deserted - 4, fatherless , mother deserted - 3, both deserted - 2, deserted by father, mother living - 10, deserted by mother, father living - 4 deserted by father, mother living but paralysed - 2. Total 107.[3] In all, she sent out 14,000 children to Canada.

Large parties, often in the care of a single matron, were packed into the restricted space on board ship, reserved for them. Unable to get in or out of their bunks in heavy seas, one of them later recorded, 'we all sicked over each other.'[4]

The Catholic Children's Protection Society first sent out a party of 50 children to Canada in May 1883. Aged between four and sixteen, they were followed by a second group of 36 in September. By 1885, the number had risen to 174. On arrival, all of these children were 'disposed of' without any difficulty. They were described as 'being drawn principally from the lowest classes of this city ... who would otherwise have most probably found their way into our reformatories or our prisons.'[5]

Mrs Lacy, matron of the Society's Home in Shaw Street, Liverpool, accompanied the children, and spent a considerable time visiting those

On Board an Emigrant Ship, at the Time of the Irish Famine.
Courtesy of National Museums Liverpool (Merseyside Maritime Museum)

previously sent out. During 1885, she reported that she had personally visited 140 children at their new homes, and in 120 cases the results were entirely satisfactory. She concluded that it was only to be expected that some of the children should not realise to the full the hopes of their benefactors.[6]

Once in Canada, the children were meant to attend school and church regularly, but the huge distances involved, and the severity of the Canadian winter, sometimes made this impossible. Some were looked upon simply as a source of cheap labour, others were adopted by their new families, and were being brought up and educated as their own children.

But by 1894, doubts were beginning to creep in. The Annual Report 'recognises the fact that where possible it is better to provide for the children in England' and of the 1,511 children who had been emigrated since the formation of the Society in 1881, 'the Committee are most careful only to take cases which would otherwise fall into the hands of Protestant societies, or who have no parents living, or whose parents have deserted them.'[7] In 1896, presumably reacting to criticism, the Report states: 'As it is sometimes asserted that children sent to Canada are abandoned, this Society preserves a watchful care over the children sent out, for three years, and often for longer.'[8]

Later reports include copies of letters sent by some of the little emigrants, to the Home in Shaw Street and to the Sisters at the Receiving Home in Canada. Most express contentment, or at least resignation to their new life, but there is a constant theme of loneliness running through them. Although the children are described as orphaned or abandoned, most seem to have had some relatives in Liverpool, and there are constant requests for information about them.

Fr Nugent had a vision of happy, healthy children, prospering in a land of opportunity; others saw it as a scheme to rid the city of those who would otherwise become a burden on the rates.

NOTES

1. Annual Reports of the Catholic Children's Protection Society (1884) p1.
2. G Wagner, *Children of the Empire* (1982) p 79.
3. Lilian M Birt, *The Children's Home Finder* (1913) p105.
4. Wagner p83 -84.
5 - 8. Annual Reports 1884 - 1900.

7

Walton Gaol's First Catholic Chaplain

The Borough Prisons Act of 1863 made it possible to have prison chaplains other than those of the Established Church. In 1864, Fr Nugent took on yet another responsibility when he was appointed the first Catholic chaplain to Walton gaol, at a salary of £300 per year. This appointment was not without opposition from the Conservative-dominated council and the Select Vestry (the equivalent of the Department of Social Services). The 'Liverpool Herald' complained: 'These men have appointed a popish priest to Walton gaol, for the purpose of preaching popery, while popery itself has been the root of the evil which sent the Romanists to prison.'[1]

Fr Nugent saw it differently: along with most temperance reformers, he saw alcohol as a fundamental cause of crime, rather than an escape from social misery. The Rev John Jones agreed: 'What a difference there would be in our town and in our gaols, if the Irish population were reclaimed from the vice of drunkenness'.

TABLE 3   Number of Roman Catholic prisoners in the borough gaol during the year 1864.

male	2,738	% born in Ireland	57%
female	3,083	% born in Ireland	63%

Source: Rev J J Jones *The Slain in Liverpool during 1864 by drink* p50.

Fr Nugent's report for the year ending 30th September 1866 shows that the number of Catholic women prisoners still exceeded that of all other denominations.

TABLE 4   Places of birth of Catholic prisoners committed during
the year ending 30th September 1866.

Place of birth	males	%	females	%
Ireland	1,060	49.9	1,386	61.5
Liverpool	808	38.0	616	27.3

Source: *Liverpool Council Proceedings, Prison Minister's Report
(1866) p581*

He attributed this humiliating fact to two causes: 'First, drink is
frightfully on the increase in Liverpool among women, especially
amongst girls from 15 - 20. If an ignorant girl once takes to drink,
and comes constantly to gaol, she soon casts off all sense of shame,
becomes bold and defiant in vice, and abandons herself to every form
of crime.'[2]

The second cause, he thought, was the lack of suitable employment for
women. Over half the women prisoners were illiterate; they tried to
make a living by street trading, and were imprisoned for obstructing the
highway. In a typical year, 308 women were committed for this offence,
65 for overcrowding,[3] and 38 widows were imprisoned for their son's
truancy from (industrial) school. For more serious offences such as
prostitution, Fr Nugent advocated even longer sentences as a deterrent:
'I have frequently found women of this class who have been in gaol 30,
40, 50, times, yet they were not more than 26 or 27 years of age.'[4]

During the year ending 30th September 1867, there was an increase in
the total number of commitments, of 1,130, and of this number 1,044
were Catholics. Fr. Nugent's explanation was ingenious: he thought
that this could be at least partially accounted for 'as previous to your
appointing two services on the Sunday, at least 10% of the Catholics
entered themselves as Protestants to escape the dreary, monotonous
solitude of Sunday in their cells' [5]

Unlike drunkenness and illiteracy, poverty was not generally seen as a cause of crime, rather as a sign of moral weakness. The poor were poor through self-indulgence and immorality. As if to underline this, Rev Jones compared family 'A' with family 'B'. Both lived in identical, adjoining houses and earned similar salaries. But whereas family 'A' was industrious, clean, sober and God-fearing, family 'B' was feckless, slovenly, habitually drunk and Irish. However, for whatever reasons, the overall trend in both violent crime and drunkenness was downwards during the last quarter of the 19th century.[6]

At the end of 1885, Fr Nugent resigned as chaplain of Walton Gaol after 'a stretch of 22 years' and proceeded to devote his energy and labours to a work most dear to him, namely caring for homeless, destitute children. In the light of his own experience, he was firmly convinced that the only remedy for crime was to 'nip it in the bud'. It was useless to attempt the reformation of hardened and confirmed criminals.[7]

He then took a well-earned holiday in Madeira.

NOTES

1. *Liverpool Herald,* 14th May 1864.
2. Liverpool Council Proceedings (LCP), Prison Minister's Report (1866) p581.
3. Overcrowding: ie allowing unmarried persons of opposite sexes to sleep in the same room.
4. LCP, Prison Minister's Report (1874) p494. In the year 1866, 9,109 prisoners could neither read nor write, and only 253 could read or write well. By 1885 the figure was still too high, viz 8,778 and 387. LCP Report of the Watch Committee on drunkenness and crime (1885) pp768 - 70.
5. LCP Prison Minister's Report (1867) p640.
6. C Emsley *Crime and Society in England 1750 - 1900* (1996) p49. 'At last the figures for drunkenness and associated crimes begin to fall.' LCP Report of the Watch Committee (1885) p768.
7. *Liverpool Daily Post* 1st January 1886.

An artists impression of a street scene,
first published in the Illustrated London News in 1877

8

Total Abstinence

During the third quarter of the 19th century, drunkenness reached epidemic proportions in Liverpool. In the year ending 30th September 1874, 12,464 men and 7,866 women were proceeded against for being drunk and disorderly.[1] Margaret Simey writes: 'Drunkenness in Liverpool achieved a degree unsurpassed anywhere in the UK and was long awarded a high place in the causes of poverty.'[2]

Believing in the policy of a free market regulating itself, Liverpool magistrates licensed public houses practically on demand, their only criteria being that the licensee should have a sufficient character and suitable premises. The number of licensed premises already operating in the neighbourhood was irrelevant. They argued that, as the industry would be self-regulating, there would not be a corresponding rise in drunkenness, but rather the reverse.

By 1865, the number of licensed premises was 2,912, with the majority situated in the poorer areas of Liverpool, and frequented by those least able to afford it. The MOH explained:

'It is no unusual thing to see these people before six o'clock on a Monday morning, crowding round the pawnshops waiting for them to open, so as to raise money from clothes or anything they can carry. As soon as it is obtained, away they go to the public house, and seldom leave till all is spent.'[3]

In the district of Vauxhall, there were 76 public houses and gin shops, and 51 beer shops, or one for every 23 families,[4] and in the area of

Lace Street alone, there were four public houses, four spirit vaults, and a brewery.

Beer was cheaper to buy than tea or coffee, and safer to drink than milk or water. The public house was often more welcoming than home, especially a home that contained a drunken wife, and where there was often no dinner at dinner time. 'Why then', asked the Rev J J Jones, in his book *The Slain in Liverpool during 1864 by Drink,* 'should the husband return to his family, when there stands on every corner, another home, in which he is always welcome?'[5]

Fr Nugent had long been aware of the problem. He knew the part drink played, and the temptation that the poor Irish were subjected to in Liverpool, after their terrible experiences of the Famine.[6] He had watched them closely: 'A little girl is sent to the public house for a quart of ale, or half a pint of whiskey. Who has the first sip? The child, of course. Girls, as well as boys thus acquire a taste for drink. There have been women sent to gaol', he said, 'who have sold every stitch they had upon them for drink, except for their chemise, and when they have got that far, they have sold the very hair off their head.'[7] Alcohol was also responsible for many suicides and fatal accidents. The most common cause of death was given as falling down cellar steps, which for the most part, were unguarded.

Along with most other parish priests, Fr Nugent had administered the temperance pledge to those of his parishioners who needed it. Rev J J Jones was aware of this when he wrote: 'There are, in Liverpool, 60 Roman Catholic priests, and every one of them administers the temperance pledge to those for whom it is a necessity.' He gave an example from his own experiences: 'Here is a little wounded child. Oh, how its little head has been battered. But how came the mishap? One day, the little one's father, returning home from the public house, seized the fire-irons and dealt out that fearful blow. Now he is reformed, for he has taken the pledge.'[8]

Still Fr Nugent hesitated for many years before he committed himself to the onerous task of establishing the Total Abstinence League of the

A Public House near the North Hay Market, Great Homer Street, 1900.
Courtesy of the Liverpool Records Office, Liverpool Libraries

Cross. He had been influenced by the work of Fr Mathew of Cork, founder of the temperance movement. Fr Mathew came to Liverpool in 1843, during his tour of England. He is said to have enrolled 600,000 people into the Movement in three months. John Denvir described how the publicans' trade fell away for a while afterwards.[9]

It was not until 1872 that Fr Nugent founded the Catholic Total Abstinence League of the Cross, during his period as chaplain at Walton Gaol. There he administered the pledge to 539 men, and 369 women prisoners, although he had no means of knowing how far they kept it once they were released.[10]

By 1875, Fr Nugent was able to purchase land at the corner of St Anne Street and Rose Place, on which to build a League of the Cross hall which could seat some 2,000 people. It was regularly packed with the poorest of the population. Each weekend he organised a concert to draw the people away from the attractions of the gin palaces and the beer shops. Each abstainer made the following pledge: 'I promise to abstain from all intoxicating drinks, except used medicinally, and by order of a medical man, and to discountenance the cause and practice of intemperance.' He then received a medal to wear.

The turn of the century brought a healthier attitude to alcohol, which was strengthened by new laws. The need for the League declined, and it did not long survive its founder.

NOTES

1. LCP, Report on the Police Establishment and the State of Crime (1874 -5).
2. M Simey *Charitable Effort in Liverpool in the 19th Century* (1951) pp25 - 26.
3. LCP, Report on the Health of Liverpool by the Minister of Health, BWS Trench (1866 - 7) p448.
4. Hume, pp15 - 16.
5. Rev J J Jones *The Slain in Liverpool during 1864 by Drink* (1865) p19.6.
6. The Famine changed everything; poetry, music, dancing, stopped. When times improved, these things never returned as they had been. Irish Folklore Commission (1945).
7. LCP, Prison Minister's Report (1866) pp200 - 02.
8. Jones, p60.

9

The Social Evil

The Watch Committee's crusade against immoral houses, in 1890 - 91, brought cries of protest from local dignitaries, who feared that if these premises were raided, they would simply open up again in other areas, possibly in respectable neighbourhoods. What they wanted was for this social evil to be kept out of sight, not eradicated.

Nevertheless, magistrates ordered the immediate closure of 300 disorderly houses, 818 persons were prosecuted for keeping immoral houses, and hundreds of destitute women were thrown on the streets.

The total number of brothels in the borough was conjectural, as the police had no power to enter them. In 1885, the number of suspected brothels was 440, containing about 1,165 women supposed to be prostitutes.[1] They recruited their clients in the numerous public houses and beer shops. Alcohol played a major role in the lives of these women. Many had turned to prostitution in order to support their addiction to drink. This, together with the desperation and misery of their lives, in filthy, overcrowded slums, was seen, by some more perceptive perhaps, as largely responsible for them taking to the streets in the first place. Others were of the opinion that women's natural sinfulness was to blame, along with indolence, love of dress and amusement, and dislike of hard work.

Refuges for fallen women were already set up in the larger towns. Their purpose was to reclaim the women for society, so of course they were selective in whom they admitted; women under 25 years old, not too steeped in vice, neither pregnant nor diseased, reasonably intelligent (many were simple-minded), and amenable to the harsh discipline

TABLE No. 12.—Showing the Number of WOMEN supposed to be PROSTITUTES TAKEN INTO CUSTODY and SUMMARILY CONVICTED for being DISORDERLY in the STREETS, during the year ending the 29th September, 1884—showing also the Number of Times for each during that period.

NUMBER OF TIMES	TAKEN INTO CUSTODY								TOTAL PERSONS	TOTAL ARRESTS	SUMMARILY CONVICTED								TOTAL PERSONS	TOTAL CONVICTIONS
	Not known to have been in Custody prior to 30th September, 1883.				Known to have been in Custody prior to the 30th September, 1883.						Not known to have been in Custody prior to the 30th September, 1883.				Known to have been in Custody prior to the 30th September, 1883.					
	13 to 16.	16 to 21.	21 and upwards.	TOTAL.	13 to 16.	16 to 21.	21 and upwards.	TOTAL.			13 to 16.	16 to 21.	21 and upwards.	TOTAL.	13 to 16.	16 to 21.	21 and upwards.	TOTAL.		
Once	...	46	366	411	...	3	700	703	1114	1114	...	25	248	273	...	2	682	684	956	956
Twice	...	10	103	113	...	2	310	365	426	932	...	3	68	75	...	...	351	351	426	852
Thrice	...	...	33	33	...	...	232	232	265	795	...	...	22	22	...	...	207	207	229	687
Four	...	...	13	11	...	...	131	131	164	676	...	...	12	12	...	...	118	118	130	520
Five	...	1	8	9	...	...	101	101	110	550	...	1	7	8	...	...	98	98	106	530
Six	...	...	...	...	...	...	71	71	71	426	...	...	...	...	...	...	60	60	60	360
Seven	...	...	2	2	...	...	40	40	42	294	...	...	3	3	...	...	24	24	27	189
Eight	...	...	2	2	...	...	20	20	22	156	...	...	...	...	...	...	11	11	11	88
Nine	...	...	...	...	...	...	14	14	14	144	...	...	3	3	...	...	13	13	16	144
Ten	...	...	3	3	...	...	9	9	12	120	...	...	...	...	...	...	7	7	7	70
Eleven	...	1	...	1	...	...	10	10	11	121	...	1	...	1	...	...	3	3	4	44
Twelve	...	...	...	...	...	...	6	6	4	72	...	...	...	...	...	...	4	4	4	48
Thirteen	...	...	...	...	...	...	2	2	2	26	...	...	...	...	...	...	...	...	...	...
TOTAL	...	67	538	585	...	5	1701	1706	2291	5586	...	32	363	395	...	2	1578	1580	1975	4282

TABLE No. 13.—Gives the Number of PERSONS who were DRUNK when APPREHENDED, their COUNTRIES, and the BRIDEWELLS at which the Charges were made.

OFFENCES	APPREHENSIONS.			BIRTH PLACE OF PERSONS Apprehended.								BRIDEWELLS AT WHICH THE PRISONERS WERE BOOKED										
	Males	Females	TOTAL.	Liverpool.	England, other parts of	Ireland.	Scotland.	Wales.	Isle of Man	Foreign Countries	Main Bridewell	Cheapside Street.	Collingwood Dock.	Athol Road.	Rose Hill.	Prescot Street	Olive Street.	Essex Street.	Hornsworth Dock	Argyle Street	Warren Street	Derby Road
Drunk and Disorderly	6350	5024	12103	6103	1461	2162	435	272	99	2567	274	867	429	1464	2671	693	211	279	596	740	1256	564
Drunk and Incapable	1968	911	2879	1063	445	380	137	109	24	103	734	54	113	264	348	214	149	68	109	296	367	80
Drunk and Assaulting Police Constables	847	124	215	435	128	165	18	20	4	17	149	43	48	110	123	44	31	52	38	35	53	43
Drunk and other Assaults	161	54	215	113	34	40	11	22	...	101	7	7	21	28	4	3	2	8	12	16	6	...
Drunk and other Offences	804	1141	1445	597	346	348	62	54	6	35	350	75	50	126	164	77	45	18	12	156	156	89
TOTAL	10359	7258	17997	8357	3621	3199	663	468	94	4123	184	690	1396	3324	1024	515	329	503	1251	2008	741	

52

so often found in these places. Of course, they also had to repent of their sinful way of life, most, if not all, Refuges being run by religious organisations.

One exception to this rule was Mrs Josephine Butler, who fought a one-woman crusade for the repeal of the Contagious Diseases Acts. [2] In 1866, she began by filling her Liverpool home with diseased and consumptive prostitutes. Before they died they were encouraged to embrace religion, in the hope of final pardon and mercy. For those fortunate enough to recover their health, Josephine opened a House of Rest, but was soon overwhelmed by sheer numbers, not only of prostitutes, but of homeless women, widows, orphans who had fought off starvation by selling in the streets, or who had been discharged from the Liverpool workhouse and had nowhere else to go. Almost half were Catholics, mainly Irish. As well as caring for them, Josephine could not resist trying to convert them to her own brand of Protestantism.

The most vulnerable group of all was children, sold into prostitution, sometimes by their own parents. In exposing this scandal, Josephine helped to achieve the raising of the age of consent for girls from 13 to 16 years.[3] The journalist, Hugh Shimmin, was particularly concerned about the number of very young girls being lured into prostitution. He notes: 'Seen on the landing-stage on a Sunday night, among the crowds of young people who habitually gather there at weekends, gaudily dressed, lower class, one of our great public men (no name given), partially drunk, was seen talking to a very young girl - a child, or little more - and by the eight o'clock boat, they crossed to Seacombe.'[4]

Fr Nugent had been created a Monsignor by the Vatican, in recognition of his untiring work among the poor of Liverpool. Now, in 1891, he found another cause, among the outcasts of Victorian society. His concern was the number of Catholic women walking the streets. His experiences as chaplain of Walton Gaol had given him an insight into the causes of prostitution. What they needed, he thought, was a place of safety, where they could be weaned off alcohol, and re-integrated into society.

He looked for help, and found it in Mother Magdalen Taylor, foundress of the Poor Servants of the Mother of God. On receiving his request, so urgent that she was obliged to reply by telegram, she accepted at once the responsibility of managing a Refuge, in Liverpool, similar to one the Order already had in London for penitent women. Fr Nugent was gratified: 'Mother Magdalen', he said, 'is a large lady; she has a large mind; but she has a still larger heart.'

The first, temporary, Shelter was set up in Limekiln Lane, off Sylvester Street, under the driection of the Sisters. Fr Nugent was anxious to comply with all Mother Magdalen's wishes. When told that she objected to the name 'The Saviour's Home' he immediately had it changed to 'St Saviour's Refuge'. Each evening it opened its doors at six o'clock, and provided supper and a night's lodgings, and breakfast, for up to 50 women. By the time of Fr Nugent's death in 1905, 19,338 homeless women had passed through, not all prostitutes, some just destitute and in moral danger.[5]

His next objective was to raise the money for a permanent Refuge. He organised public meetings at local venues, where he spoke movingly, to packed audiences, on the subject of 'incorrigible women - what are we to do with them?' Only once was he carried away by his own rhetoric, when he described the streets of Liverpool as paved with Irish prostitutes.

Aided by generous donations from the usual sources, ie the merchants and businessmen of the city, of all denominations, he raised enough money to purchase the former public baths and wash-houses on the corner of Bevington Bush and Paul Street for £1,500, and to have it fitted out as a steam laundry with room for 50 poor girls 'who have gone astray', at a total cost of at least £7,000.[6]

Fr Nugent was justly proud of his Refuge; he invited most of the local clergy, and his benefactors to visit, including the Pope's Delegate, who said Mass for the Sisters. As it was funded by public subscription, he was anxious to show the good work being done at the Refuge, by publishing an account of interesting cases. On being told of this, Mother Magdalen said that she wished the Sisters to do all in their power for the girls' souls and bodies, but to make no reference to their sad past. When he heard her wishes Fr Nugent said: 'Well, that is best', and no account was ever kept.[7]

The Refuge was intended, eventually, to be self-supporting, and to provide its inmates with a trade when they left. It was open to all, irrespective of creed. However, non-Catholics would be transferred to an institution of their own denomination; Fr Nugent could never be accused of proselytising. A night portress was on duty throughout the night to admit any poor, homeless woman or girl, so that she would not need to be on the streets overnight. When Fr Nugent (as he still preferred to be called) died, it had given training to 2,213 women. How many of the poor creatures stayed the course, and re-emerged into society to lead a more virtuous life, we shall never know.

NOTES

1. LCP Report of the Watch Committee (1885) pp768 - 70.
2. J Jordan *Josephine Butler* (2001) The Contagious Diseases Acts of 1864, 1866 and 1869 were meant to tackle the alarming rate of venereal disease among the armed forces, by the registration and supervision of prostitutes, and their compulsory detention in special hospitals if diseased. Growing opposition, mainly from women, led to the Acts being suspended in 1883, and finally repealed in 1886.
3. A report published in 1857 states there were at least 200 'regular' prostitutes under the age of 12 in Liverpool. F Finnegan *Poverty and Prostitution* (1979) p81 n.
4. Hugh Shimmin *Porcupine* vol 1, no 1 (1860) p129.
5. Bennett, pp115 - 6.
6. Mgr James Nugent *Proposed Refuge and Shelter for Women (Paul Street)* 25th November 1891.
7. *Mother as We Knew Her 1871 - 1900* pp117 - 118 (unpublished).

RESCUE THE FALLEN !

ST. SAVIOUR'S REFUGE
18, LIMEKILN LANE,
LIVERPOOL.

Courtesy of SMG Archives, St. Mary's Convent, Brentwood.

10
SINGLE MOTHERS

For a long time, Fr Nugent had collected newspaper cuttings on cases of infanticide. He was horrified at the number of child murders in the local press. For years, infant mortality in Liverpool had remained at a high level, and the 'Liverpool Daily Post' reported: 'Anyone who doubts this has only to witness the numerous funerals of infants, which take place simultaneously every Sunday afternoon.' The chances of illegitimate children surviving was even lower, and the suicide rate among unmarried mothers correspondingly higher as, rejected by their families, they were unable to bear the shame heaped on them by 'respectable people'. The bodies of newborn babies were often found in trunks in left-luggage offices, or in rivers. Verdicts of murder were usually returned against 'person or persons unknown'. Some were left on doorsteps or in church porches, in the hope that someone would find them before it was too late.

In Liverpool, during the year ending 30th June 1862, inquests were held on 81 smothered infants. A very large proportion of these were slain on Saturday nights and Sunday mornings by drunken parents. The journalist Hugh Shimmin remarked: 'Anything which will draw the mothers away from seeking their sole enjoyment in drink will prove the most effectual check to smothering of children ... but it is worthwhile thinking what is to be done to stay the plague in the meantime.'[1]

Nothing was done, however, and the problem quickly got worse. During the year 1864, 143 children died from suffocation, three-quarters of these between Saturday and Monday, and 13 between 24th and 31st December.[2]

In his capacity as chaplain of Walton Gaol, Fr Nugent had been in a unique position to study the problem of infanticide, and his opinion was sought by many in authority. Until then, he said, he was under the impression that the women on the streets very rarely had children, but such was not the case. It was not uncommon for a woman to have had two or three children, and all these were generally 'sided', ie got rid of, within 12 months of their births, either through neglect, or by overlaying.

During the year 1884, over 150 infants under one year died, many of them from these causes. Ellen Carr's baby died in this way on 25th December 1884. At its wake the room caught fire and the baby's body was badly damaged, while the drunken mourners lay asleep on the floor. The Coroner's jury returned a verdict of accidental death. The editor of the 'Liverpool Review' thought that the burial club money was often a temptation to parents.[3]

The first Infant Life Protection Act, which was passed in 1872, was ineffective due to lack of officers to implement it. In 1897, another Act, meant to remedy the defects of the first, suffered the same fate. The Children's Act of 1908 made a drunken parent, who slept with a child under three, who subsequently died of suffocation, liable for its death.

In 1897, at the advanced age of 75, Fr Nugent bought a house in Dingle Lane, Toxteth Park, and opened it as a Home for unmarried mothers and their babies. This was the fulfilment of a long cherished ambition to help a section of the population for whom nothing had been done. His action attracted the attention of the local press. The opening ceremony was reported admiringly by the 'Liverpool Daily Post' under the headline: 'Monsignor Nugent's Philanthropic Work - A New Departure'. This was a vast improvement on the Press's attitude of 30 years earlier.

The Home was put in the charge of Mary Magdalen Taylor of the Poor Servants of the Mother of God, 'who have realised so great a measure of success in Mgr Nugent's Refuge for fallen women in Limekiln Lane.'

The building, named the House of Providence, comprised some thirty apartments, and accommodated 60 inmates.

In his opening speech, Fr Nugent revealed his anguish:

'For 30 years he had had in his mind the desire to check, in some way, the terrible destruction of infant life that was going on in the city, the extent of which few could realise; there was no source of accurate facts. Within the walls of Walton Gaol, he had learnt many means by which infant life could be destroyed, how many an injured girl, who had strayed for the first time, turned to infamy, from which her whole being recoiled, in order to find food and shelter for herself and her babe. These facts had urged him to make an effort. She should be taken by the hand, and cared for, in the hope and trust that she might sin no more.'[4]

The House of Providence was open to all, regardless of creed. Only first-time mothers were admitted. They were allowed to stay for a year after the birth of their babies. As far as possible, the father was forced to contribute to the support of his child (a startling innovation). The chief support of the Home was its laundry until, in 1898, Fr Nugent launched his quarterly magazine, 'Rescue Notes', in order to attract subscriptions and donations towards the upkeep of the Home. However, its appearance was irregular, and it ceased publication soon after Fr Nugent's death. However, in 1903, he had persuaded Archbishop Whiteside to begin an annual collection, in order to provide support for the House of Providence and other Homes in the archdiocese. The House of Providence continued its work until after the 2nd World War, by which time attitudes to single mothers were changing.

NOTES

1. Hugh Shimmin, *Courts and Alleys of Liverpool* (1864) pp134 - 145.
2. J J Jones, *The Slain in Liverpool During 1864 by Drink* (1865) p23.
3. *Liverpool Review* 10th January 1885. Infant burial clubs were popular among the poor.
4. *Liverpool Daily Post* 17th February 1897.

Source: annual Reports of the Registrar General.

Figure 2.2. The long-term trend of infant mortality (seven year moving mean) in 22 towns, 1840-1910.

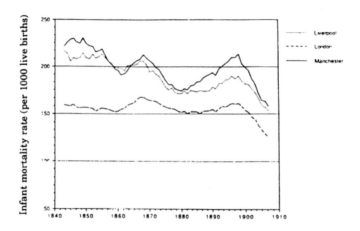

Although the civil registration of births, marriages and deaths in England and Wales was established in 1837, many births went unregistered until 1874, when penalties for not complying were introduced.

11
THE END

In the spring of 1903, Fr Nugent returned from yet another fund-raising trip to the United States. It had had to be curtailed because of his failing health. Whilst he was away, his many friends had planned a banquet at the Adelphi Hotel, Liverpool, both to welcome him home, and to mark the appreciation in which he was held by his fellow citizens.

Arch Bishop Whiteside proposed the toast: 'The guest of the evening.' Fr Nugent, replying, said that he was overwhelmed at the honour done to him that evening by men of many different religious beliefs. He was now 82 years of age, and to whatever length his life might be spared, he hoped to spend it in Liverpool. 'I belong to Liverpool, and with God's help I intend to die in Liverpool.'

Alderman Louis Cohen, a non-Catholic, replying, said that he thought a site should be selected where a statue could be erected to commemorate one of Liverpool's greatest citizens. All classes and all creeds thought well of Fr Nugent and wanted a lasting memorial of his work, even before he died, and that was how the project of a statue of Fr Nugent got under way.

The idea was taken up enthusiastically by the press and public of the city. Money poured in from all directions, but before the statue could be erected, Fr Nugent died, on 27th June 1905.

At his death, the 'Liverpool Daily Post and Mercury' filled nine columns with obituary notices. The following extract is typical of the style: 'At the final farewell ... the Monsignor's face seemed lit with radiance, with expectation of a bliss beyond the tomb, while he bowed his silvered head in resignation and content, before the inevitable decree.'[1]

Pontifical High Mass at St Nicholas Pro cathedral (the church in which he had been baptized, and ordained priest, 50 years before) was celebrated by the Rt Rev Dr Whiteside, Bishop of Liverpool, assisted by Mgr Canon Carr. Throughout the city, flags flew at half mast. Thousands of people lined the streets around Copperas Hill, and the route to Ford cemetery, or looked down on the scene from the windows of adjoining houses. Memorial cards of Fr Nugent were sold in the streets.

Last word goes to *Rescue Notes* p9. 'He has passed beyond our praise or criticism now, and the good he accomplished lives after him.'[2]

NOTES

1. *Liverpool Daily Post and Mercury* 28th June 1905.
2. *Rescue Notes* 1906. No p9.

Memorial Statue to the Late Monsignor Nugent.

Erected by Public Subscription in St. John's
Gardens, Liverpool.
Unveiled, 8th December, 1906.

Courtesy of the Liverpool Records Office, Liverpool Libraries

MEMORIAL STATUE TO LATE MONSIGNOR NUGENT

On 8th December 1906, in the presence of a huge gathering of all sections of the community, the bronze, life-sized statue of Monsignor Nugent was erected in St John's Gardens, Liverpool. It shows him in the robes of a monsignor, with his left hand on the shoulder of a ragged boy, and his right hand raised in benediction. It stands on a square stone pedestal, on the four sides of which are engraved as follows:-

MONSIGNOR JAMES NUGENT
1822 - 1905
Erected by public subscription
Unveiled December 8th 1906
'SAVE THE BOY'
'An eye to the blind, A foot to the lame, The father of the poor.'
His words:- 'Speak a kind word, take them gently by the hand. Work is the best reforming and elevating power. Loyalty to country and to God.'
The Apostle of Temperance. The protector of the orphan child. The consoler of the prisoner. The reformer of the criminal. The saviour of fallen womanhood. The friend of all in poverty and affliction.

RIGHT REV. MONSIGNOR JAMES NUGENT.
Born March 3rd, 1822.   **R. I. P.**   Died June 27th, 1905.

Courtesy of the Liverpool Records Office, Liverpool Libraries

Father Nugent

BIBLIOGRAPHY

UNPUBLISHED PRIMARY SOURCES
Sisters of the Poor Servants of the Mother of God, *Mother as we knew her* Reminiscenses of Mother Foundress, written by Sisters who knew her personally, 1871 - 1900

PUBLISHED PRIMARY SOURCES
Liverpool Record Office. Liverpool Council Proceedings 1865 - 1885.
Annual Reports of the Catholic Children's Protection Society 1884 - 1900
Foundations of the Sisters of Notre Dame in England and Scotland from 1845 - 1895 (1895)
Nugent Mgr James, Proposed Refuge and Shelter for Women (Paul Street) November 25th 1891
Parliamentary Papers 1852 - 3 LXXXIX (1690)

SECONDARY SOURCES
Armstrong R A, *The Deadly Shame of Liverpool* (1890)
Belchem J, *Liverpool in the Year of Revolution: The Political and Associational Culture of the Irish Immigrant Community in 1848* in J Belchem (ed) *Popular Politics: Riot and Labour. Essays in Liverpool History 1790 -1940* (1992)
Bennett J O, *Father Nugent of Liverpool* (1949)
Birt, Lilian M, *The Children's Home Finder* (1913)
Brady L W, *T P O'Connor and the Liverpool Irish* (1983)
Burke T, *Catholic History of Liverpool* (1910)
Denvir J, *Life Story of an Old Rebel* (1910)
Devas F C, *Mother Magdalen Taylor - Foundress of the Poor Servants of the Mother of God* (1927)
Emsley C, *Crime and Society in England 1750 - 1900* (1966)

Finnegan F, *Poverty and Prostitution* (1979)
Frazer W M, *Duncan of Liverpool* (1934)
Gauldie E, *Cruel Habitations: a History of Working Class Housing 1780 - 1918* (1974)
Grey-Edwards Rev A H, *A Great Heart* (1906)
Grisewood W, *The Poor of Liverpool* (1899)
Harrison B, *Drink and the Victorians* (1971)
Hume, Canon A, *Missions at Home, or a Clergyman's Account of the Town of Liverpool* (1850)
Jones, Rev J J, *The Slain in Liverpool During 1864 by Drink* (1865)
Jordan J, *Josephine Butler* (2001)
Midwinter E, *Old Liverpool* (1971)
Miller A, *Poverty Deserved?* (1988)
Neal F, *Sectarian Violence - The Liverpool Experience 1819 - 1914* (1988)
Rimmer J, *Yesterday's Naughty Children* (1986)
Shimmin H, *Courts and Alleys of Liverpool* (1864)
Shimmin H, *Liverpool Life* 2nd series (1857)
Simey M, *Charitable Effort in Liverpool in the 19th Century* (1951)
Wagner G, *Children of the Empire* (1982)
Waller P J, *Democracy and Sectarianism: A Political and Social History of Liverpool 1868 - 1939* (1981)
Walton J & Wilcox A, *Low Life and Moral Improvement in Mid-Victorian England: Liverpool Through the Journalism of Hugh Shimmin* (1991)
Weddel M, *Child Care Pioneers* (1958)
Wohl A S, *Endangered Lives (*1983)

JOURNALS
Cathedral Record 1949
Rescue Notes Christmas 1906
Xaverian 1853, 1894

NEWSPAPERS
Liverpool Courier
Liverpool Daily Post and Mercury
Liverpool Herald
Liverpool Journal
LIverpool Review
Liverpool Porcupine

Father Nugent